YOUR PASSPORT TO

FRANCE

Charly Haley

raintree

a Capstone company — publishers for children

Raintree is an imprint of Capstone Global Library Limited, a company incorporated in England and Wales having its registered office at 264 Banbury Road, Oxford, OX2 7DY – Registered company number: 6695582

www.raintree.co.uk
myorders@raintree.co.uk

Edited by Jamie Hudalla
Designed by Colleen McLaren
Original illustrations © Capstone Global Library Limited 2021
Originated by Capstone Global Library Ltd
Printed and bound in India

978 1 3982 0551 2 (hardback)
978 1 3982 0552 9 (paperback)

British Library Cataloguing in Publication Data
A full catalogue record for this book is available from the British Library.

Acknowledgements
We would like to thank the following for permission to reproduce photographs: iStockphoto: Gregory_DUBUS, 23, serts, 24; Red Line Editorial: 5; Shutterstock Images: Anatoly Tiplyashin, cover (flag), Catarina Belova, cover (bottom), Everett - Art, 9, FrimuFilms, 14, Hung Chung Chih, 6, kan_khampanya, 13, Leonard Zhukovsky, 28, Natashadub, cover (map), Radu Razvan, 27, s4svisuals, 19, Stefano Ember, 20, Takashi Images, 16
Design Elements: iStockphoto, Shutterstock Images

We would like to thank Céline Brossillon, Assistant Professor of Modern Languages at Ursinus College, USA, for her assistance in the preparation of this book.

Every effort has been made to contact copyright holders of material reproduced in this book. Any omissions will be rectified in subsequent printings if notice is given to the publisher.

CONTENTS

Words in **bold** are in the glossary.

CHAPTER ONE

WELCOME TO FRANCE!

The Eiffel Tower shines over France's capital city, Paris. This tall metal tower lights up at night. More than 7 million people visit it every year.

The Eiffel Tower is one of many famous places in France. France is a country in western Europe. More than 65 million people live there. Most of them speak French. Some speak English too. France has many **immigrants** from north Africa. They often speak a language called Arabic.

People from all over the world love to visit France. The country has many **monuments** and museums that show its rich history. Many of these places are in Paris. People also visit France's beaches, mountains and countryside.

MAP OF FRANCE

Giverny
PARIS
Eiffel Tower ▲■▲ The Louvre
▲ Palace of Versailles
Colmar

FRANCE

N
W ◆ E
S

■ Capital City
● City
⬡ Landform
▲ Landmark

Marseille
Nice

Explore France's
cities and landmarks.

When the weather is good, people sit on the lawn by the Eiffel Tower.

FRENCH CULTURE

Food is a big part of French **culture**. French people take their time shopping for fresh ingredients and eating meals. Many people go to outdoor markets for fresh foods, such as fruit and vegetables. Some vendors sell their food every day, while other markets might happen once a week.

FACT FILE

OFFICIAL NAME: ....FRENCH REPUBLIC
POPULATION: 65,097,000
LAND AREA: ....543,965 SQ. KM (210,026 SQ. MI)
CAPITAL: ....PARIS
MONEY: ....EURO
GOVERNMENT: ....ELECTED PRESIDENT
LANGUAGE: ....FRENCH

GEOGRAPHY: Located in western Europe, France borders Spain, Belgium, Luxembourg, Germany, Switzerland and Italy. It also borders the Atlantic Ocean, the Mediterranean Sea and the English Channel. Most of the north and west parts of the country are flat. Southern France has mountains, including the Alps and Pyrenees. France has islands, such as Corsica, off its coasts.

NATURAL RESOURCES: France is one of the countries that make the most wind energy. This means it uses wind to make electricity. France also has a lot of coal mines in the north.

France is known for its art, fashion and more. The country hosts the famous Tour de France bicycle race. Many French people show their pride by sharing their history and culture in their various museums.

CHAPTER TWO

HISTORY OF FRANCE

In the 770s, King Charlemagne ruled over the area that is now France. He took control of other parts of western Europe too. He wanted people to come together and practise Christianity. Early French kings made this religion a big part of their **governing**.

THE FRENCH REVOLUTION

Louis XVI and his wife, Marie Antoinette, were among the last kings and queens. Their rule ended in 1792 after French citizens took over the government.

JOAN OF ARC

France was in a war for 116 years in the 1300s and 1400s. It was called the Hundred Years War. An 18-year-old woman called Joan of Arc led part of the French army. She helped win a major battle in 1429. Joan of Arc became famous across France. But a year later, an English leader of the Catholic church said she was a witch and had her killed. Today Joan of Arc is a beloved figure of France.

Marie Antoinette was famous for her love of fashion.

TIMELINE OF FRENCH HISTORY

768–814: King Charlemagne rules the area that is now France.

1429: Joan of Arc leads a French army to victory during the Hundred Years War.

1643–1715: King Louis XIV rules France.

1774–1792: King Louis XVI and Marie Antoinette are king and queen of France.

1787–1799: People fight to overthrow the monarchy during the French Revolution.

1804–1815: Napoleon Bonaparte rules France, with an interruption from 1812 until 1815.

1814–1824: King Louis XVIII rules France.

1914–1918: France fights in World War I.

1939–1945: France fights in World War II.

6 JUNE 1944: Britain and the United States fight against German troops in France on D-Day, a decisive battle in the war.

1958: France elects President Charles de Gaulle and creates the form of government that it still has today.

1993: France and other countries create the European Union. This is a group of European countries that work together.

2017: France elects Emmanuel Macron as president.

This takeover was part of the French Revolution. The revolution lasted more than 10 years. People fought for a more **democratic** government because they felt the king and queen had too much power and did not treat the people fairly.

In the early 1800s, France had a military leader called Napoleon Bonaparte. He led the country in many wars. After Napoleon's rule ended, France had different leaders. Some were kings, while others were presidents elected by citizens.

FRANCE IN THE WORLD WARS

In the 1900s, France fought in World War I and World War II. During World War II, Germany **invaded** and took over France. British and US forces landed in France to help the French. This invasion, on 6 June 1944, is known as D-Day. It changed the war. Germany was defeated in World War II a year later.

In 1958, France formed the government that it still has today. The country elected President Charles de Gaulle. Presidents can stay in office for 2 terms, or 10 years.

FACT

During World War II, Germany took control of France's government. French people who continued to fight the Germans were called the French Resistance.

CHAPTER THREE

EXPLORE FRANCE

France is a popular country for **tourists**. Paris is one of the top 10 most visited cities in the world. It has many sites to explore.

FACT
Tourists enjoyed visiting Notre Dame Cathedral in Paris. But in April 2019, a large fire damaged the beautiful building. Experts say it could take two decades to repair.

Visitors can get a beautiful view of the city from the top of the Eiffel Tower. There are more than 600 stairs to the second floor. The tower looks over the River Seine, which flows through Paris.

ROAD TO THE ARC DE TRIOMPHE

The Champs-Elysees is a famous street in Paris. It is known for its shopping and entertainment options. The street has many high-fashion clothes shops. It also has restaurants and cinemas.

Visitors can climb 284 steps to get a view of Paris from the top of the Arc de Triomphe.

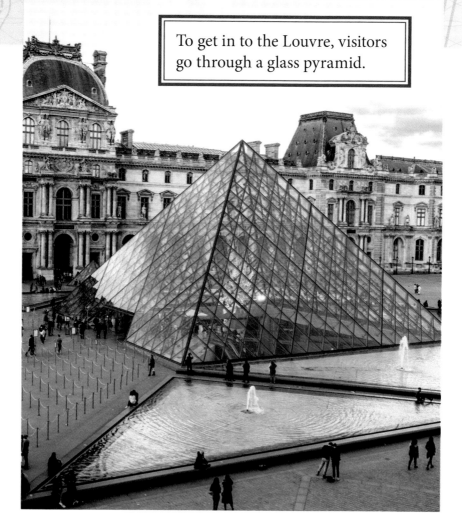

To get in to the Louvre, visitors go through a glass pyramid.

The Arc de Triomphe is the start of the Champs-Elysees. This large stone arch is at the centre of a roundabout in the street. France's government started building the arch in 1806 to honour those who lost their lives in battle.

MUSEUMS AND GARDENS

The Louvre, a popular art museum, also sits along the River Seine. More people visit it than any other art museum in the world. The Louvre houses many famous paintings, including the *Mona Lisa*. The museum has sculptures, drawings and many other pieces of art.

The Tuileries gardens are outside the Louvre. They have beautiful flowers and trees. The gardens also have statues and ponds.

Paris has many more gardens and parks. One of the largest parks is the Bois de Boulogne. This used to be a place where French kings hunted. Now it is a park for visitors. It has forest areas, lakes and a waterfall.

FACT

The Bois de Boulogne is 850 hectares (2,100 acres). That is bigger than 1,000 football pitches.

The most famous room in the Palace of Versailles is the Hall of Mirrors. It has 357 mirrors!

A GOLD PALACE

The Palace of Versailles is just outside Paris. Louis XVI and Marie Antoinette lived there. So did other French kings and queens. Now it is open to visitors. Versailles is known for its priceless art and decorations. It also has one of the largest gardens in the world. Workers at the palace plant more than 210,000 flowers a year!

People who like castles can visit the Loire Valley in central France. Tourists enjoy several castles and the beautiful countryside.

CITIES ON THE COAST

France has beautiful beaches. Cities in the south, such as Marseille and Nice, are on the Mediterranean Sea. Along with beaches, these **coastal** cities have museums, markets and other places to visit.

SMALL TOWNS

Many people enjoy visiting France's beautiful small towns. One popular small town is Giverny. Giverny was home to Claude Monet, a famous painter who lived in the early 1900s. Tourists can visit his house and see the gardens he painted.

CHAPTER FOUR

DAILY LIFE

Daily life in France is not so different from Britain. People go to school and work. The school year for French children is from September to June. They get July and August off for the summer holidays. The school day starts at about 8.30 a.m. and ends at about 4.30 p.m. School children typically get a two-hour break for lunch. Some go home during that time.

THE SOUND OF BELLS

In cities and **rural** areas, people can listen to the beautiful chime of bells. Bells from old churches ring throughout the day. Some bells ring once every hour. People can listen to them while they relax outdoors at cafés.

FACT

The French are known for their fashion. Paris Fashion Week is one of the biggest fashion shows in the world.

A bell tower rises high above the town of Saint-Tropez.

People often sit outside cafés.

In these public spaces, **etiquette** is important. Many French people value respectful language and manners.

FRENCH MEALTIME

Food is important to French people. Their dinners often take a long time, since they have three courses instead of one. Dinners might include a starter, the main dish and dessert. Meals are a time for friends and family to talk with each other. It is a French tradition to appreciate long mealtimes.

French food is famous around the world. Many cheeses come from France. French breads are common too. They bake long breads called baguettes and flaky pastries called croissants.

CROQUE MONSIEUR

With an adult's help, you can make French food at home. This sandwich is popular at French cafés. It is often served with bechamel sauce.

Sandwich ingredients:
- bread (two slices)
- ham
- cheese
- butter

Bechamel ingredients:
- 70 g butter
- 32 g plain flour
- 950 ml milk
- 1 teaspoon salt
- ¼ teaspoon freshly grated nutmeg

Sandwich method:

1. Put ham and cheese between the two slices of bread.
2. Heat a frying pan on the hob over medium heat. Melt the butter in the pan.
3. Fry sandwich for 3 to 4 minutes on one side. Flip and fry other side.

Bechamel method:

1. Melt butter in a saucepan over medium heat.
2. Stir in flour. Let it cook until it is golden.
3. Turn heat to medium-high and whisk in milk.
4. Turn down heat to medium-low and let it sit for 10–20 minutes.
5. Add salt and nutmeg.
6. Spread sauce on sandwich.

CHAPTER FIVE

HOLIDAYS AND CELEBRATIONS

Some holidays are unique to France. One is Bastille Day. It is on 14 July. During this holiday, the country remembers the people who lost their lives during the French Revolution. There are parades and fireworks. People dance and eat together.

NATIONAL CELEBRATIONS

France observes Armistice Day on 11 November. In the UK we do this too, and we call it Remembrance Day. The holiday honours the soldiers who died in World War I. Some people wear black on this day. Parades show appreciation for the armed forces.

France celebrates May Day on 1 May. May Day recognizes workers. Many businesses close.

Bastille Day is sometimes celebrated with red, white and blue fireworks, the colours of the French flag.

The town of Colmar is famous for its Christmas markets.

On May Day, people give each other flowers called lilies of the valley. They relax with family.

RELIGIOUS HOLIDAYS

Christianity has a long history in France. About half of the French population still practises a form of Christianity called Catholicism. This means Christian holidays such as Christmas are widely celebrated in France. Many businesses and schools close for Christmas. People of other religions live in France too. A small number of French people practise Islam. They celebrate *la fête de la rupture*, or Eid al-Fitr. This period of three days follows a month spent fasting from sunrise to sunset. People enjoy big meals together during Eid al-Fitr.

CHAPTER SIX

SPORT AND RECREATION

French people enjoy many sports, and France even hosts famous sporting events. One of the most famous is the Tour de France. It is a bicycle race across the country. Athletes from around the world take part in it. The race takes three weeks. It covers about 3,470 kilometres (2,162 miles). The race started in 1903. At that time, most of the cyclists were French.

The Tour de France has grown into a worldwide event. People from faraway places such as Costa Rica and Australia participate. About 20 teams of 9 riders race. Each year, people around the world watch it on TV. Some people travel to France to watch the race in person. There are parties across the country to celebrate it.

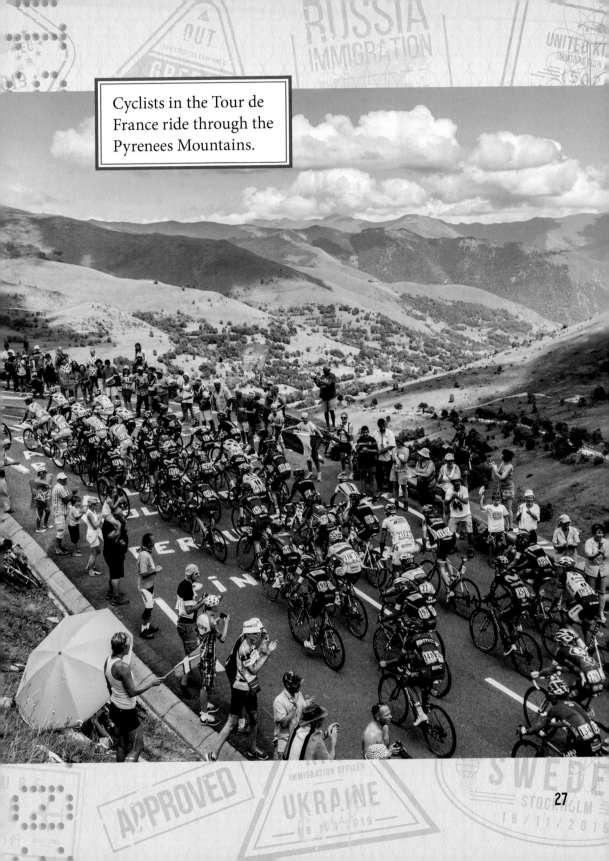

Cyclists in the Tour de France ride through the Pyrenees Mountains.

The French Open is the only Grand Slam tournament played on clay.

TENNIS AND FOOTBALL

France also hosts the French Open. This is one of the world's largest professional tennis tournaments. Tennis players from around the world compete.

Football is the most popular sport in France. More than 2 million people play football in France. Many more watch it on TV. The French national team won the World Cup in 2018.

ESCARGOT

Escargot is a traditional French game. It is the French word for snail, pronounced "ess-car-go". The game is like hopscotch. You just need some pavement chalk and a small group of people to play.

1. Use the chalk to draw a circle on the ground.
2. Draw a line coming out of the circle like a spiral wrapping around it.
3. Draw lines to divide the spiral into squares. Write a number on each square.
4. The first player hops in the spiral on one foot. The player hops on as many squares in a row as he or she can. The players cannot touch the lines. If the player makes it to the circle, he or she can pick any square. The player writes his or her name on it. Now no other players can hop on that square.
5. Players take turns. As more players make it to the circle, more squares will have names on them.
6. The game is complete when every square has a name on it. The winner is the person with the most squares.

Winter sports are very popular in France. People go skiing and snowboarding in the mountains. France is known for its sports, art and more. Its food and fashion are famous. Many people visit the country. From castles to the Eiffel Tower, France is full of beautiful sites to see.

GLOSSARY

coastal
near the coast, by the sea

culture
way of life for a group
of people

democratic
having to do with a system
of government in which
people vote on the way the
country is run

etiquette
polite behaviour in society

govern
run or rule a state,
organization or country

immigrants
people who have come into
another country to live
there permanently

invade
enter a country or state
with the aim of taking
control of it

monument
statue or building that is
made to remind people of a
person or event in history

rural
relating to the countryside

tourist
person visiting
another country

FIND OUT MORE

BOOKS

Christmas in France (Christmas Around the World), Jack Manning (Raintree, 2017)

Paris (City Trails), Lonely Planet Kids (Lonely Planet Kids, 2016)

The Culture and Recipes of France (Let's Cook!), Tracey Kelly (Raintree, 2020)

WEBSITES

www.bbc.co.uk/bitesize/topics/zyhp34j/articles/zhw7vk7
Watch this BBC Bitesize video about life in France.

www.bbc.co.uk/programmes/p0114qpv
This BBC video explores what it is like to live in Paris.

www.natgeokids.com/uk/discover/geography/countries/facts-about-france
Find out more about France with National Geographic.

INDEX

OTHER BOOKS IN THIS SERIES

YOUR PASSPORT TO CHINA
YOUR PASSPORT TO ECUADOR
YOUR PASSPORT TO EL SALVADOR
YOUR PASSPORT TO ETHIOPIA
YOUR PASSPORT TO IRAN
YOUR PASSPORT TO KENYA
YOUR PASSPORT TO PERU
YOUR PASSPORT TO RUSSIA
YOUR PASSPORT TO SPAIN